# Evangelism: Easy As 1, 2, 3

## Pastor Floyd Hughes

Evangelism: Easy As 1, 2, 3
Copyright © 2023 Floyd Hughes

Printed in the United States of America

ISBN-979-8-9875164-0-9

# Dedication

This book is dedicated to pastors of small congregations who labor regularly to share the Gospel in their communities. No other company or organization is doing as great a work in your community as you.

# Table of Contents

# Introduction

This book is not a comprehensive resource for every question or Bible verse regarding evangelism. It is just a step-by-step guide to help equip Christians to do the main thing God has called us to do—share the Gospel. Also, this introduction is the longest one I have ever written for any of my books, but I feel like this is one of the most important books since it deals with evangelism. Therefore, it deserves a more detailed introduction.

I make a lot of videos about Christianity and post them on social media. I don't do it to gain a following. I do it to engage and to interact with others and answer their questions. One of my greatest passions (next to comic books, movies, and, well, making videos) is finding creative ways to share the truths of God's Word with people. That's what I do with the videos I post on social media.

At CrossRoads, the congregation I pastor, we teach through books of the Bible. We also do topical preaching—preaching and teaching about a specific topic and what the Bible says about it. However, my primary teaching focus is through books of the Bible. But I absolutely love when I can capitalize off of both teaching styles. For example, throughout the summer of 2022, we taught through the book of 1 John.

After teaching through 1 John, I did a topical teaching on evangelism. It makes sense that if you preach about loving others and living a God-honoring life, the primary theme of 1 John, you should probably preach about why the Church, the body of Christ, exists. It exists to share and show the love of Christ to the people within our circles of influence. Those are the people we see and interact with regularly or daily: local cashiers, crossing guards, the attendant in the doctor's or dentist's office, co-workers, family, and friends.

## TikTok Made Me Do It

For those who are thinking, where is this going, and what is this introducing? Let me explain. I do a lot of live videos to answer questions from people. One of the biggest reasons people are deconstructing (questioning their faith or leaving their congregations) is because they aren't getting truthful answers to their questions.

I do a live Q and A (question and answer session) with three other pastors as a part of *Faith Pittsburgh* on Facebook. Shameless plug, we put out a Christmas devotional called *Unwrapping Christ at Christmas*; it's available on Amazon, so you can easily add that to your reading list. I also do a weekly prayer livestream on Facebook and two live Q and A sessions on TikTok. If it hasn't become clear, I believe answering questions about Christianity, God, and the Bible is vital to being a pastor.

On the live Q and A sessions on TikTok, I talk about evangelism, you know, because it's supposed to be the primary focus of the Church. Then I pray with people and answer questions about Christianity, the Bible, and whatever. Quite a few questions usually center on the Green Lantern ring I wear, but most are about God and the Bible. Since most of the New Testament epistles are responses to questions, I feel like most pastors should be willing to answer questions. I'm not hating on those who don't. I'm just saying it's biblical, and that's why I do it.

For those who still don't see where this is going, here you go. On the Thursday night live Q and A on the last week of preaching through the evangelism series, I asked if anyone would be interested if I turned the evangelism series into a book to help equip Christians to share the Gospel within their circles of influence. I stated that I would make it inexpensive to buy a printed copy of the book on Amazon and free, or as close to free as Amazon would allow, for the Kindle edition.

There was an overwhelming interest except from the haters and atheists who always seem to find time to join Christian livestreams. Several people suggested I also write a children's version of the book. The interest in that was even more favorable. The consensus was that a book focused on the practical aspects of evangelism would be great, but a companion children's edition would be priceless.

It's important to note that children helped to develop the children's edition and the toddler's picture book that make up this series.

They were then reviewed and approved by Christian ministry teachers. The proceeds from the children's versions go directly to the children who helped write and review the books. I want them to reap the rewards of their efforts.

So, that's what this book is about—inspiring and equipping Christians to return to our evangelical roots of sharing the Gospel. If you're reading this and feel that you are already prepared to share the Gospel, then hopefully this will encourage you to keep sharing the Gospel with folks in your circles of influence.

Also, consider giving a copy of this book to a family member or friend who you think would benefit from reading it. If you or they have children, consider purchasing one of the children's editions as a gift for them. After all, everyone loves children's books.

If you're reading this and have questions about God, Christianity, or the Bible, there are some options to help you. Check out the *Faith Pittsburgh* Facebook page and share any questions or topics you want the panel of pastors to address. Listen to the *Faith Responders Podcast* and message us with any questions or issues you want Pastor Mark Berkshire and me to address. You can also check out my live Q and A sessions and feel free to ask questions.

If you have specific questions about evangelism after reading this book, feel free to contact me. You can message me via social media, email me, or comment on any of the myriads of videos I post online. As I've stated, I'm passionate about sharing the truths of God's Word and engaging with Christians so we can be better equipped to do God's will. And at the very core of what God wants the Church, the body of Christ, to do is tell others about His Son, Jesus Christ, what the Bible calls evangelism.

# What Is Evangelism? It Is What It Is... Until It Isn't

**[16] And they went with haste and found Mary and Joseph, and the baby lying in a manger. [17] And when they saw it, they made known the saying that had been told them concerning this child.** – *Luke 2: 16 – 17 (English Standard Version)*

Unfortunately, one of the reasons many Christians aren't involved in evangelism regularly is because we have been given an incorrect definition of evangelism. It probably wasn't intentional, but it still happened. Raise your hand if you've been told that evangelism is one of the following:

- o *Evangelism is leading people to Christ*. Although people may accept Christ through someone's evangelical efforts, leading them to Christ or leading them in a prayer to accept Christ is not the biblical definition of evangelism. There's nothing wrong with doing that; it's just not the biblical meaning of evangelism. However, many pastors, denominations, and congregations mistakenly led people to believe that if you don't lead a person to Christ via prayer, you're not doing biblical evangelism. That's not true. It's okay if you do lead a person in prayer. But that's not the definition of evangelism.

- *Evangelism is inviting someone to the Sunday Celebration*. This is not evangelism; it's just being a good Christian. There is nowhere in the Bible where evangelism is defined as inviting people to the Sunday Celebration. In fact, most of the biblical accounts associated with evangelism have nothing to do with the Sunday Celebration. Again, nothing wrong with inviting the people in your circles of influence to join you at a local congregation to celebrate Jesus, but that's not evangelism. That's good local congregational outreach, but it's not evangelism.

○ *And speaking of local congregational outreach, <u>our spaghetti fundraisers and Easter egg hunts are not evangelism</u>.* All the events we do to bring people into the building or raise funds for a new roof are not evangelism. Some of the events may be considered congregational outreach but not evangelism. And to be clear, anything we do to get people to join our congregations or attend a Sunday Celebration is not evangelism. Nothing wrong with doing it, but it's not evangelism. It's just local congregational or community outreach, which we all should do, but it's not evangelism.

By now, you're fully versed on what actions are not evangelism. You might also be wondering, What is the biblical definition of evangelism? The word evangelism comes from the Greek word used regarding the birth of Jesus in Luke chapter 2 verse 10.

When the angel appeared to the shepherds, he told them he was bringing good news for all the people. The good news was that the Savior of humanity was born. The Greek word for the phrase good news was *euangelizo,* from which we derive the English word evangelism. That's where the word comes from, but the concept of evangelism comes from what the shepherds did in verses 16-17.

They checked out what they had been told, found it to be true, and told others what had been said to them. Take note, they didn't tell others what they saw—a baby in a manger. They told others what had been said to them about the baby in the manger: the good news or the Gospel that the Savior of humanity had been born. This is the definition of evangelism, telling those we know about Jesus.

## What Does Evangelism Look Like

Engaging in evangelism really boils down to one of three aspects, and it will look different for different people. The three aspects of evangelism are 1.) telling others about Jesus, 2.) sharing the Gospel of Jesus, or 3.) telling others what God has done in our lives either through or because of Jesus. That's it.

Although these three aspects sound similar, they have slight variations. But you know what they all have in common? They all involve telling others about Jesus. That's the heart of evangelism. That will help determine whether or not what we are doing is evangelistic.

Telling others about Jesus will look different for many people. For some, it might be telling people that He really lived and died just like Peter did in his speech in Acts chapter 2. Although many of the people Peter spoke to knew of Jesus, they didn't know the truth about Jesus. Peter shared the truth of who Jesus was with them. That's evangelism.

Whilst some people may be comfortable telling others about Jesus, not many people will be comfortable sharing the Gospel of Jesus as Paul did in 1 Corinthians chapter 15 verses 1 - 8. In verse 1, Paul stated that his goal was to remind the readers of the Gospel. The word he used for Gospel is the same Greek word used in Luke 2 for good news. Paul went on to say that the good news, or the Gospel, is that Jesus died for our sins in accordance with the Scriptures, was buried, and then was resurrected on the third day in accordance with the Scriptures. He went on to say that Jesus was seen after His resurrection by all of the apostles multiple times and by at least 500 witnesses.

For those who are wondering, this good news doesn't conflict with the good news that the angels shared with the shepherds. In Luke 2, the good news was that the Savior of humanity was born. Here, Paul shares how Jesus saved humanity. That's sharing the Gospel of Jesus Christ. That's evangelism.

Granted, some people may feel that only a pastor, a missionary, or someone in full-time ministry can share the Gospel, as outlined above, with people. I've heard some people say they don't want to mess it up or that they don't want to share something that isn't true. But this aspect of evangelism can be shared by everyday people with folks in their circles of influence.

You don't have to be in full-time ministry to do it, and you don't have to memorize the verses in 1 Corinthians to do it. You just need to know that Jesus died for our sins in accordance with the Scriptures, was buried, then resurrected three days later in accordance with the Scriptures, and was seen by hundreds of people. That's the Gospel of Jesus Christ. Sharing that with people in your circles of influence is evangelism.

## The Most Common Type of Evangelism

However, the aspect of evangelism that most people will be comfortable sharing is what God did in their life through Jesus. The shorter version is here is what Jesus has done for me. If you're a Christ follower, you likely have a testimony about what Jesus has done in your life. If the word testimony seems daunting or intimidating, just think of a struggle Jesus has brought you through, a journey He helped you stay on, or a roadblock He helped you overcome. Anything you share about what Jesus has done in your life is evangelism.

Because we all likely have some testimony about what Jesus has done in our life, either small or large, this is the most comfortable and most straightforward aspect of evangelism for many people. Because it's the most comfortable, one would think that this aspect of evangelism would be taking place every day in homes, inside or outside of workplaces, inside or outside of schools and college campuses, and in every community. But we all know that's not happening.

Another point of clarification, evangelism is not about forcing our beliefs on others or beating people over the head with a Bible or Bible verses. It is the crystal-clear call throughout the Bible to proclaim the truths of God to all people. In Psalm 105 verse 1, the psalmist writes that we should praise God and proclaim his Name so that all nations know what He has done.

In Acts chapter 13, Paul and Barnabas told the people that God commanded them to bring salvation to the Gentiles by sharing God's Word. The Gentiles who heard them say this responded by honoring the Word of God and became believers, and the Word of God spread through the entire region. That's evangelism.

And now that we know exactly what evangelism is, we can see how easy it is for anyone to do because it's as easy as 1, 2, 3.

# Step 1 of Evangelism: MC Hammer Was Right, You've Got to Pray

**⁴And while being in their company *and* eating with them, He commanded them not to leave Jerusalem but to wait for what the Father had promised, Of which [He said] you have heard Me speak. ⁵For John baptized with water, but not many days from now you shall be baptized with (placed in, introduced into) the Holy Spirit. – *Acts 1: 4 – 5 (Amplified Bible, Classic Edition)***

Yes, MC Hammer was right in his song entitled "You've Got To Pray". The first step of evangelism is prayer. But so help me God, I will go to my grave saying he was not right about the parachute pants. I'm not judging him. I'm just stating a fact; no one was right about parachute pants (especially the white ones with sparkles that I wore a few times).

But just as Christians should pray regularly and daily, praying about evangelism has to be a regular practice. Evangelism should start with prayer because it needs to be led by the Holy Spirit. When we lead evangelistic efforts, we end up with spaghetti fundraisers and Easter Egg hunts. We end up with actions that focus on our congregation or denomination or getting people into our buildings rather than focus on Jesus Christ and proclaiming His Name.

Probably one of the most incredible evangelistic events in the Bible wasn't initiated by men but by the Holy Spirit as directed by Jesus. It shows why prayer should always be the first step of evangelism. In Acts chapter 1, the resurrected Jesus was eating with the disciples. He directed them to wait for the outpouring of His Holy Spirit so they could become His witnesses.

Think about what Jesus was saying. They had already seen, spent time with, and had meals with the resurrected Jesus. They could have told countless people about Jesus, and they probably did. But Jesus instructed them to wait until they were filled with the Holy Spirit before they went out to evangelize. Their response shows why they and we need to be led by God's Holy Spirit.

Their response was about their needs, their desires, and their earthly situation, whether the nation of Israel would be restored. Their focus wasn't proclaiming the name of God or being witnesses for Jesus. They focused on their needs and wants, which they thought were important. That is why evangelism needs to be led by God's Holy Spirit. That is why we need to pray.

Fast forward to Acts chapter 2 (or depending upon your Bible size, just turn the page). The disciples were praying as Jesus directed them. Once they were filled with God's Holy Spirit, look at the difference. When confronted, everything they said pointed back to Jesus, His kingdom, and how the people could be a part. Although Peter referenced the history of the people of Israel, it was only to show them how it all pointed to Jesus.

# There Is a Difference

Just to be clear, and so you can see I am not making this up, let's compare the responses of the disciples. First, let's look at the response of the disciples in Acts chapter 1, before they were filled with the Holy Spirit:

**4 On one occasion, while he was eating with them, he gave them this command: "Do not leave Jerusalem, but wait for the gift my Father promised, which you have heard me speak about. 5 For John baptized with water, but in a few days you will be baptized with the Holy Spirit." 6 Then they gathered around him and asked him, "Lord, are you at this time going to restore the kingdom to Israel?" *(New International Version)***

Now look at the response of the disciples in Acts chapter 2 after praying and being filled with the Holy Spirit to be witnesses of Jesus:

**[36] "Therefore let all Israel be assured of this: God has made this Jesus, whom you crucified, both Lord and Messiah." [37] When the people heard this, they were cut to the heart and said to Peter and the other apostles, "Brothers, what shall we do?" [38] Peter replied, "Repent and be baptized, every one of you, in the name of Jesus Christ for the forgiveness of your sins. And you will receive the gift of the Holy Spirit. [39] The promise is for you and your children and for all who are far off—for all whom the Lord our God will call." *(New International Version)***

In Acts chapter 1, their focus was on their needs, their congregation, their nation, and how they could grow their numbers. Our focus would likely be the same. But in Acts chapter 2, with the Holy Spirit leading, their focus was all about Jesus. That's what our focus will likely be if we allow the Holy Spirit to direct our evangelical efforts.

Evangelism needs to be led by the Holy Spirit so that we don't make it about us, our congregations, or our denominations. If we are led by God's Holy Spirit, the same Spirit that raised Jesus from the dead, then the Holy Spirit can guide us in ensuring our evangelistic efforts focus on proclaiming the Name of Jesus and bringing people into God's kingdom instead of focusing on bringing them into our congregations.

In case you are not used to praying about evangelism, the last chapter of this book is devoted to it. Yes, prayer is the first step of evangelism, but it's also a foundational part of evangelism. And it's a crucial part of step 2.

# Step 2 of Evangelism: Be Willing to Share The Good, The Bad, and The Ugly

[37] "And that's why I'm singing—I, Nebuchadnezzar—singing and praising the King of Heaven: "Everything he does is right, and he does it the right way. He knows how to turn a proud person into a humble man or woman." - *Daniel 4: 37 (The Message)*

To fully grasp the second step of evangelism, I need to reiterate the basic definition of evangelism and the aspect of evangelism to which most people will gravitate. Evangelism is sharing about Jesus Christ. The different aspects of evangelism are telling others about who Jesus is, sharing the Gospel of Jesus, or telling others what God has done in our lives either through or because of Jesus. Most people will be more comfortable sharing about what Jesus has done in their life.

Step 1 of evangelism is to pray so the Holy Spirit can guide us so we can ensure the focus is on Jesus and not us. Step 2 is a little more personal. If we share what Jesus has done in our lives, then we must be willing to share the good, the bad, and the ugly. That's another reason why step 1 is so important—so that the Holy Spirit can guide what we share in step 2.

Right now, some of you are probably thinking, Wait a minute. Does that mean I have to share ___? And ___? And when I did ___ to someone? And even when God healed me from ___?!?!? The answer to those questions is not going to come from me but from the Holy Spirit. Or another way to say it, see step 1, pray about it, and let the Holy Spirit guide you.

## It Isn't Going to Be Easy But...

Sometimes telling people about what God has done in our lives can be easy to do. It is a lot easier to share the "look what God brought me out of" or the "look what God brought me through" or the "look what God helped me overcome" moments. Other times it can be painful, humbling, and even humiliating. In all instances, we have to trust God will guide us in what to share and how much to share.

A great example of this is in chapter 4 of the book of Daniel. In that chapter, Nebuchadnezzar, the ruthless narcissist who was the king of Babylon whom Daniel worked for, shared his testimony. Granted, Nebuchadnezzar didn't share what Jesus did for him, but he did share the experience of how God humbled him. There was a very slow progression of Daniel sharing with Nebuchadnezzar about God before Nebuchadnezzar acknowledged God as being sovereign over his own life.

And although Daniel wasn't sharing about Jesus (although later in the book, the angel Gabriel did share with Daniel about the coming of Jesus the Messiah), Daniel was prayerfully evangelizing by communicating with the people in his circles of influence about God. The people in his circles of influence just happened to be governors and kings.

In chapter 2, Daniel revealed what Nebuchadnezzar had dreamed without being told the dream and then revealed what the dream meant. To this, Nebuchadnezzar responded, "Surely your God is the God of gods and the Lord of kings and a revealer of mysteries, for you were able to reveal this mystery." (See Daniel 2:47 *NIV*). He didn't accept God as his god, but he did acknowledge Him as the God of gods.

In chapter 3, Nebuchadnezzar and his government officials saw God save the lives of Shadrach, Meshach, and Abednego from a blazing furnace. This time Nebuchadnezzar responded, "Praise be to the God of Shadrach, Meshach and Abednego, who has sent his angel and rescued his servants! They trusted in him and defied the king's command and were willing to give up their lives rather than serve or worship any god except their own God. Therefore I decree that the people of any nation or language who say anything against the God of Shadrach, Meshach and Abednego be cut into pieces and their houses be turned into piles of

rubble, for no other god can save in this way."
(See Daniel 3:28-29 *NIV*).

Some theologians agree that God didn't save them just to prevent them from dying. They believe God saved them so Nebuchadnezzar could see God at work and put his faith in God. And although Nebuchadnezzar acknowledged that God could save physically, he didn't recognize his own need for spiritual salvation.

In chapter 4, Nebuchadnezzar acknowledged his narcissism and acknowledged God as sovereign over all kings and kingdoms, including his kingdom and himself. He started by sharing how great God is and that God's kingdom is eternal. Then he shared how God got him to that place. It is humbling for someone who prides themself on, well, themselves, to share something like this.

This behavior was a significant change since previously Nebuchadnezzar had equated himself with the gods. He had even elevated himself above the gods, including Daniel's God, who Nebuchadnezzar had acknowledged was above all gods. In verses 13-15 of chapter 3 of the book of Daniel, Nebuchadnezzar threatened Shadrach, Meshach, and Abednego and told them no god would be able to save them from him. He was essentially saying there was no god that could save them from him, his actions, and his decree to cast them into the fiery furnace because his actions were above or greater than all gods.

However, in the next chapter, this same Nebuchadnezzar shared a rather embarrassing, humbling, and humiliating experience. He shared how God humbled him. He didn't just share it with a few people, with a few advisors, or with close family members and friends. Instead, he made a public proclamation.

He didn't just make a Facebook post about it that only friends and family would see. He made what equates to a public address that would be carried on every TV station, live streamed worldwide, and audio clips played on every radio show in today's culture. Also note, if it were today's culture, his political opponents would make fun of him and criticize him, and late-night TV hosts would bash and ridicule him. But that didn't stop him from sharing his testimony.

God isn't asking us to make a state of the nation public address to the world of our most humbling moments. He is asking us to be willing to share what He has done in our lives through His Son, Jesus Christ. For some, that may mean sharing with someone about an addiction that Jesus helped them overcome. For others, it might actually mean sharing something humbling with someone else. For most of us, it is going to be sharing the good things that Jesus has done and the roadblocks He has helped us overcome.

## A Little Can Go a Long Way

Although Nebuchadnezzar shared a lot of what God did for him, a woman that Jesus spoke to by a well shared just two sentences. In John chapter 4, the Apostle John recorded how Jesus had to go through Samaria. After stopping by a well, Jesus had a conversation with a woman in which Jesus told her that He knew about some of the broken relationships in her past. Jesus was also aware of her current relationship, which wasn't in line with the faith she was professing.

Read the entire passage of Scripture for yourself because there is a lot more to the conversation. Jesus didn't just walk up to the woman and call her out for the way she was conducting her love life. In fact, nowhere in that passage did Jesus condemn her for it. He merely used the opportunity to reveal Himself to her as the Messiah, the Christ, the one whom she admitted would come and reveal all truth.

The woman left Jesus, went back to town, and told people, "Come, see a man who told me all that I ever did. Can this be the Christ?" (See John 4:28-29 *ESV*). That's it. That's all she said to the townspeople, but their response to her two sentences is why we need to do evangelism. Verse 39 states that many people from the town believed in Jesus because of her two sentences. That's a massive accomplishment for just two sentences.

She didn't go into detail about what she and Jesus spoke about. She didn't tell anyone about the broken relationships in her life that Jesus knew about. She merely told people what Jesus had done in her life. That's evangelism.

It's great when we can share the good things that Jesus has done, but like Nebuchadnezzar, we have to be willing to share some of the uglier moments in our lives. That doesn't mean we have to go into detail. It means we pray about it so we know what to share and how much to share. That's why step 1, or prayer, is a crucial part of being able to do step 2. And step 3 is...

# Step 3 of Evangelism: Go Out and Do It (Sorry, the phrase Just Do It was already copyrighted)

⁹ But God said to Jonah, "Is it right for you to be angry about the plant?" "It is," he said. "And I'm so angry I wish I were dead." ¹⁰ But the LORD said, "You have been concerned about this plant, though you did not tend it or make it grow. It sprang up overnight and died overnight. ¹¹ And should I not have concern for the great city of Nineveh, in which there are more than a hundred and twenty thousand people who cannot tell their right hand from their left—and also many animals?"
– Jonah 4: 9 – 11 (*New International Version*)

I won't rehash all the steps again, but I will reiterate step 1, prayer. Prayer is a foundational part of evangelism because it is the stepping stone for the other two steps, and it's crucial for this, the third step of evangelism. The third step is pretty easy on paper, but it is one of the hardest things for some people to do, especially if you're an introvert like me. The third step is to actually go out and do it—to prayerfully go out and share with others what God is doing in your life through His Son, Jesus Christ.

It won't matter if you're willing to share what God has done in your life if you don't go out and share what God has done in your life. God wants us to have conversations about Him outside of the Sunday Celebrations. He wants us to get to know people and share our stories and our lives with others. And He wants us to tell others about His Son, Jesus Christ.

Some people may judge us, laugh at us, and criticize us as we do so. But others may experience a new life with Jesus Christ because we go out and do it. There are eternal benefits if we, as the body of Christ, do it, if we prayerfully go out and share our stories. However, there are also eternal consequences if we don't.

As stated previously, this doesn't mean that we go out and beat people over the head with a Bible. It also doesn't mean that we start being disrespectful by bombarding people with our testimony and our stories if they aren't interested or willing to listen. Nor does it mean criticizing or judging folks who may not share their stories with others.

What it does mean is that we follow the steps. We prayerfully share our stories with people with whom the Holy Spirit inspires us to do so, and we do it respectfully. Step three is vital because, again, there are eternal benefits for others when we do actually go out and share what God is doing in our lives. And again, there are eternal consequences if we don't.

## Hi My Name Is Jonah

One of the best examples of why it is so important that we go out and do it is in the book of Jonah. The book of Jonah is probably one the most evangelical books in the Bible, second only to the book of Acts. (That's just my two cents, which isn't worth much since we are still in a coin shortage.) Although most people focus on the portion of the book of Jonah that deals with the whale, that's not the most important part.

What's truly important is the lengths that God was willing to go to in order to have Jonah share God's word of salvation and repentance with people who had different cultural, religious, and political beliefs than Jonah. I won't focus on the entire evangelical aspect of the book of Jonah here, but if you're interested, you can read about it in my book, *Hi My Name Is Jonah*. I share details about that book at the end of this book.

However, I will highlight God's perspective on the need for salvation that God reveals in the book of Jonah. Jonah reluctantly went to Nineveh to do what God told him to do. I use the word reluctantly, well, because he was reluctant. God had to call a whale to swallow Jonah, and even then, it took three days before Jonah acknowledged, "Those who pay regard to false, useless, and worthless idols forsake their own [Source of] mercy and loving-kindness. But as for me, I will sacrifice to You with the voice of thanksgiving; I will pay that which I have vowed. Salvation and deliverance belong to the Lord!" (Jonah 2:8-9 *AMPC*).

Some theologians believe the worthless idol Jonah was worshipping was his desire to keep the word of God amongst his own people. If that's true, then it makes sense that committing to take the Word of God to people with different cultural and political beliefs was a sacrifice for Jonah despite his vow as a prophet of God to share God's Word. But Jonah reluctantly went and delivered God's message of the need for repentance to the people of Nineveh.

Although he was doing God's will, Jonah didn't pray about it, and he definitely wasn't happy about it. It was just the opposite. The people of Nineveh repented at hearing God's Word. (I share specific events that led up to their repentance and why Jonah was uniquely qualified to share that message in my book, *Hi My Name Is Jonah*.)

Despite their repentance, Jonah was angry. In chapter 4, Jonah complained to God about God's mercy and compassion being shown to the people of Nineveh. God used this opportunity as a teaching moment for Jonah and us to show us God's perspective on why salvation is so important.

Jonah was sitting outside the city pouting about God's decision to show mercy to the people of Nineveh. The city was in the desert, located in what is modern Iraq today. God caused a plant to grow to provide shade for Jonah to ease his discomfort from being in the hot sun, which obviously pleased Jonah. But then God caused a worm to attack the plant, which caused the plant to dry up. By the time the sun rose the next day, the intense heat was beating down on Jonah along with a scorching wind brought on by God.

By now, some people might be thinking, wait, was God punishing Jonah for his reluctance to obey God? The answer is no, not at all. God wasn't punishing Jonah. God was revealing His reason for showing mercy to the people of Nineveh to Jonah.

God asked Jonah if it was okay for Jonah to be so upset about a plant. Jonah responded that he had every right to be angry. I absolutely love God's response because it shows God's perspective regarding the salvation of people to Jonah and to us: "God said, 'What's this? How is it that you can change your feelings from pleasure to anger overnight about a mere shade tree that you did nothing to get? You neither planted nor watered it. It grew up one night and died the next night. So, why can't I likewise change what I feel about Nineveh from anger to pleasure, this big city of more than 120,000 childlike people who don't yet know right from wrong, to say nothing of all the innocent animals?'" (See Jonah 4:10-11 *The Message*).

Although this version is more of a paraphrase, I think it accurately captures the sentiment. God hates sin and wants all people to repent. He wants all people to be recipients of His grace, mercy, and love. He wants all people to be saved from an eternity spent separated from Him. But no one will know that if the people of God don't go out and tell others.

God cared about the eternal destination of the citizens of Nineveh. It was important to Him. They were important to Him. So, despite how Jonah felt about going, God wanted Jonah to share God's Word with them.

God also cares about the eternal destination of the folks in our circles of influence. They are important to Him. He loves them just as much as He loves us. So, despite how we feel about it, God wants us to prayerfully go and share our stories with them about what God is doing in our lives through His Son, Jesus Christ, because the only way they can experience salvation is through His Son, Jesus Christ. If we are recipients of God's love, grace, mercy, and forgiveness because of the death, burial, and resurrection of Jesus Christ, why wouldn't we want others to be recipients as well?

## Do We Really Want God to Chase Us?

Granted, Jonah wasn't going out to tell others what Jesus had done in his life. But he still needed to go out and tell others about

God. Because Jonah was reluctant to do it, God had to chase Him down, send a whale to swallow him, and then use a plant and a worm to show Jonah why it was important that he go out and do it.

If you're still unsure why it was important, it's because people matter to God. What's going on in their lives matters to God. The fact that people may end up spending an eternity separated from God matters to God, and it should matter to us.

I am pretty sure God isn't going to cause us to spend a long weekend in the belly of a whale if we don't go out and do it (but I'm not God, so I could be wrong). But I'm also pretty sure there are eternal benefits for those with whom we share our stories if we (**step 1**) prayerfully (**step 2**) are willing to share what God has done in our lives, and (**step 3**) actually go out and do it.

# Prayer Summary

**¹ And he told them a parable to the effect that they ought always to pray and not lose heart. -** *Luke 18: 1 (English Standard Version)*

For those who have read my devotionals, you know I like to add a prayer at the end of each chapter. For those who haven't, a complete list of my devotionals follows this chapter. However, since prayer is such a crucial part of evangelism, I thought it best to put the prayer portion of this devotional in its own chapter.

Many people might be wondering how to pray with regard to evangelism. Should a person pray about it daily? Should a person pray about evangelism when heading to work or in situations where one might meet new people? Or should a person pray about it when they think about it? Those are all great questions with a straightforward answer—yes.

The goal isn't to change the way you pray or check off evangelism when spending time in prayer. The goal is to make praying about evangelism a consistent part of whatever your prayer life looks like today. That is going to look different for everyone.

If you have a regular daily prayer time, then as a part of that prayer time, ask God to help break down any walls of separation that might keep you from sharing what God is doing in your life. Pray that God leads you to people with whom your specific story will benefit. Ask God to reveal what to share and how much to share. Pray for God to inspire you to actually do it—to share your story when the Holy Spirit prompts you to do so.

Making this a regular consistent part of your prayer time will make it easier to share your story when the time comes. Even if you only pray about it when you're heading into situations where you might encounter people, this type of prayer is still applicable. To be honest, I do both.

I pray about evangelism during my prayer time, but I also pray about it before heading into situations where I might encounter new people. I don't do it because I'm super holy or anything.

I do both because I'm an introvert (granted, one who talks a lot and makes a whole lot of videos to interact with others, but still an introvert).

As an introvert, it's difficult for me to engage with people I don't know. So, during my regular prayer time, I pray about ways God can use me to help build His kingdom. But I also pray when going into the gym or grocery store or before meetings or heading into situations where I might meet new people.

Admittedly, I used to pray, "God, please keep people from talking to me." That's the unwritten prayer that most Christian introverts pray. However, now I pray that God guides any interactions or conversations I have. I also pray that His Holy Spirit will inspire me to be willing to share as much or as little of my story as needed.

Even if you only pray about evangelism when you think about it, that's still better than not praying about it at all. If you're someone who only prays when you think about it at random times, that's okay. Sidenote: Consider this a random time and pray that God would encourage you to share what He is doing in your life with all whom you are led to do so by His Holy Spirit.

That's it. That's the whole book on evangelism. It's a short book because evangelism really is as easy as 1, 2, 3. But for those who still want more, take the time to read about my other books on the following pages.

# Other Books in the Evangelism Series

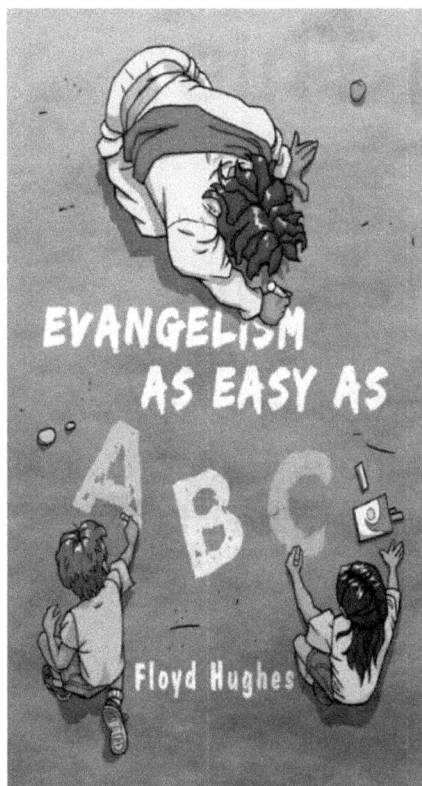

***Evangelism As Easy As A, B, C***: (The evangelism book for youth) Evangelism isn't meant to be a chore or task like homework. It is meant to be something that children do as naturally as walking, talking, or playing. In this book, written by a pastor and his 8-year-old niece, they share what evangelism means and they share three simple steps that make evangelism as easy as A, B, C.

# Coming This Spring

**The Evangelism A B Cs:** (The evangelism picture book for children) Talking to others can be as easy as A, B, C. Find out what the A, B, and C are for in this journey to learn how to tell others about Jesus and His love for them.

# About the Pastor

Floyd Hughes was born and raised in New York City. He and his wife Christina (and their furry friend Krypto) live in Jefferson Hills, a suburb of Pittsburgh, where Floyd serves as pastor of CrossRoads Community Church of Jefferson Hills. Floyd served 12 years in the US Army, worked in the telecom industry, and worked as a government consultant before becoming a full-time pastor. He is a co-host of the *Faith Responders Podcast* and a co-host of the *Naps or Nothing Moms Podcast*. He is also a contributor to the *Faith Pittsburgh Livestream*. Floyd is a self-proclaimed geek, a self-proclaimed foodie, a social media over user, and an avid comic book and movie fan. One of his favorite things to do is to find creative ways to share the truths of God's Word with people in his circle of influence.

# Other Books by the Pastor

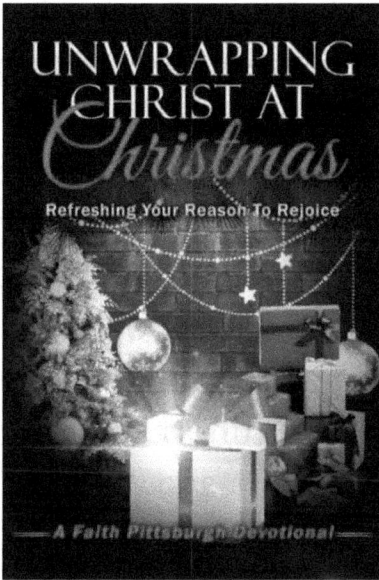

***Unwrapping Christ At Christmas: Refreshing Your Reason To Rejoice:*** This Christmas devotional is a collaboration from the pastors of *Faith Pittsburgh*. We pray it refreshes your reason to rejoice at the birth of Christ this Christmas. May it bless you and your family and may your gift giving and regifting begin with us. *Faith Pittsburgh* is a non-denominational Christian ministry that strives to inspire, educate, and support the Christian community in the Pittsburgh area.

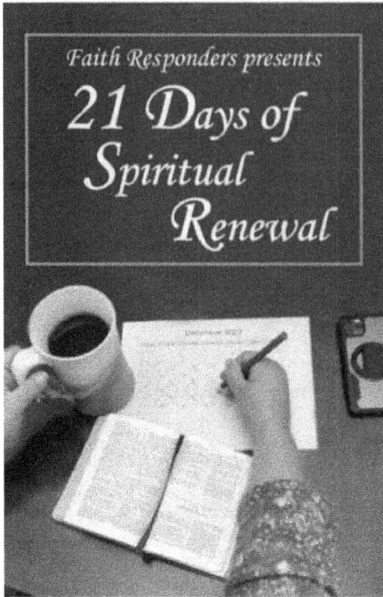

**Faith Responders presents 21 Days of Spiritual Renewal**: The past few years have been hard on many people due to the pandemic, economic hardships, and unprecedented racial and political division. How can Christians expect to strengthen their walk with God amidst such cultural chaos? In this devotional, Pastor Floyd Hughes and Pastor Mark Berkshire try to provide an answer. The pastors host the *Faith Responders Podcast*, a podcast to equip Christians to respond in God honoring ways to events happening in our culture. They bring that same spiritual insight into this devotional designed to inspire the Christ follower to strengthen and renew their faith. If you're willing to spend 2 to 3 minutes a day with God and this devotional, then in 21 days, the time it traditionally takes to break a habit, you can be on the path to spiritual renewal.

**Hi My Name Is Jonah**: The book of Jonah is probably one of the most familiar books of the Bible. Whilst many are familiar with the fish story, few are familiar with God's passionate desire for Jonah to step across racial, cultural, and political lines to share God's message of salvation and repentance. These are the same lines that many Christ-followers refuse to cross today. Although it is likely none of us will end up spending a long weekend in the belly of a large fish if we don't cross those lines, we can use Jonah's account as a prayer guide to help us break down the walls of division that are dividing our congregations, communities, and our nation. It will help us show the love of Christ to those who may not look like us, vote like us, or even share our beliefs. It will help us invite people of all cultures, races, faiths, and political perspectives to become recipients of Christ's amazing love.

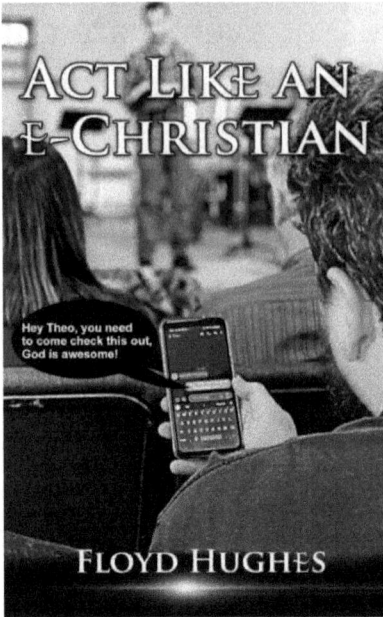

***Act Like An E-Christian***: The book of Acts is more than just a history of the early Church. It is one of the first recorded evangelical resources used to share the Gospel. Without access to the internet, Google Maps, or Facebook, Luke, the author of the book of Acts, captures over 30 years of Church history. He also captured the start of dozens of new congregations and thousands upon thousands of people's commitments to follow Jesus. Luke meticulously recorded all of this just to share the Gospel with a friend. This devotional will serve as a guide to help share the love of Christ with those in your circles of influence, show the love of Christ to them with your actions and posts, and invite them to be recipients of God's amazing love.

# A Christian Fiction Novella Coming Soon From Pastor Floyd Hughes

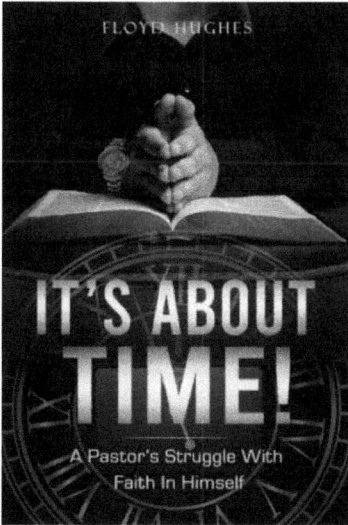

*It's About Time! A Pastor's Struggle With Faith In Himself*: It's something every pastor goes through, a crisis of faith and a question of self-worth. When Pastor Caden Roscoe began questioning his faith while serving the community to which God called him, he brought his concerns to God. God answered by taking Caden into the past to confront the issues Caden was dealing with in his own time period. God also wanted Caden to see that Caden was called by God to do more than fill a building with people on Sunday morning. He was called to transform and save a community. Caden saw firsthand, the lengths that God was willing to go to in order to equip those God called to serve and to save God's people. As he watched history unfold, Caden would see a servant of God rise up and a powerful nation fall all by God's hand. But would that be enough to help Caden overcome his lack of faith in himself?

www.ingramcontent.com/pod-product-compliance
Lightning Source LLC
Chambersburg PA
CBHW071933020426
42331CB00010B/2843